100 Ways

Increase Your Commissions

P. Fit

Disclaimer: For information only

Introduction:

The following report includes important information about becoming a super affiliate that may cause you to reconsider what you thought you understood. The most important thing is to study with an open mind and be willing to revise your understanding if necessary.

The only way to keep up with the latest about becoming a super affiliate is to constantly stay on the lookout for new information. If you read everything you find about promoting affiliate products, it won't take long for you to become an influential authority.

1. The "Best Money" Spell

Tell your prospects it was the best money you ever spent. Your prospects

have likely said the same thing about a product that they've purchased in

the past. You will likely trigger those same feelings about the affiliate

product you are promoting.

2. The "Reluctant At First" Spell

Tell your prospects that you were very reluctant at first to endorse any

product but give them a reason why this one is different. Your prospects

will think you wouldn't hurt your reputation by promoting an affiliate

product that wasn't up to your standards.

3. The "First And Only" Spell

Tell your prospects that this is the first and only product of its kind. Your

prospects will think the affiliate product is very rare. They will consider

the product to be very valuable, especially if it will give them their desired

benefit.

4. The "No Hesitation" Spell

Tell your prospects you have absolutely no hesitation recommending the

product. Your prospects will feel they better not hesitate buying your

affiliate product because if you have a great relationship with them, they will trust you.

5. The "Regret It" Spell

Tell your prospects you regret not buying the product sooner. Your

prospects will try to avoid feeling regretful and purchase your affiliate product. They know how much emotional pain can be caused by feeling any kind of regret.

6. The "Without A Doubt" Spell

Tell your prospects that, without a doubt, it is the most incredible product that you've bought in the last year. They will trust you because you are sharing specific information with them that looks and feels more credible

7. The "I Didn't" Spell

Tell your prospects that they can't lose by buying the product because you didn't. Your prospects have likely felt like losers in the past buying products that never delivered. They will want to avoid losing, especially if you can back up your claims with some proven facts.

8. The "Only My Opinion" Spell

Tell your prospects it's only your opinion but the product is amazing. Your prospects will feel it's less of a sales pitch because you are telling them it's only your opinion. They will let down their buying defenses when they aren't being sold to.

9. The "I'm Not Kidding" Spell

Tell your prospects that you're not kidding when you say the product could mean the difference between pleasure and pain. They will actually see the difference of buying and not buying the affiliate product. People usually choose the most rewarding option.

10. The "Words Can't Describe" Spell

Tell your prospects that words can't begin to describe what the product has done for you. Your prospects have likely had that feeling when something felt so good they couldn't describe it. You will likely trigger that same feeling with your statement.

11. The "Stop Now" Spell

Tell your prospects that you highly recommend them to stop what they are doing and buy the product. Your prospects will think, "This affiliate product has to be good if he's/she's telling me to stop what I'm doing."

12. The "Best So Far" Spell

Tell your prospects that you have bought plenty of products in the past but this is the best one so far. Your prospects will feel you must be really experienced at using these products so they will likely believe you and at least take a look at the affiliate product you are offering.

13. The "My Idea" Spell

Tell your prospects how frustrated you are that you didn't think of the product idea. Your prospects have likely said that same statement to themselves
in the past and will understand that the affiliate product could really benefit their life.

14. The "It Does" Spell

Tell your prospects that the product does exactly what the business says it does. Your prospects likely have bought products that never lived up to the businesses' claims. They will feel you have been through the same situation and aren't lying just to make an affiliate sale.

15. The "Thankful" Spell

Tell your prospects that you are so thankful that you decided to try out the product because of the many benefits you've received from it. Your prospects like to hear the benefits you received from the product or service. They figure if they buy the affiliate product they will get the same benefits.

16. The "Quick Rewards" Spell

Tell your prospects specifically how quickly you received the benefits of the product. Most people like to get their desired benefits fast. They lead busy lifestyles and don't want to wait long to get the desired results.

17. The "One Is Worth It" Spell

Tell your prospects that just one of the benefits of the product is worth the price. Your prospects will consider the affiliate product to be of good value when you say just one benefit is worth the price of the product.

18. The "Worth More" Spell

Tell your prospects the product is worth way more than the price that it's being offered for. Your prospects will consider the affiliate product or service to be a good bargain. They will feel like they are getting more than their money's worth.

19. The "10 Out Of 10" Spell

Tell your prospects that you rate the product 10 out of 10. Your prospects usually consider the number or symbol '10' as being the best rating a product can get. They have been branded their whole life to look at ratings of certain products or services before they buy.

20. The "I Was Skeptical" Spell

Tell your prospects you were skeptical about the product at first but you definitely made the right decision buying it. Your prospects have likely been skeptical about products in the past too. They will understand where you are coming from and buy since you built a little rapport.

21. The "Buying Wish" Spell

Tell your prospects you wish you had bought the product before buying a similar product. Your prospects will think they should buy the product too before they do something else that would jeopardize their lifestyle and the benefits they crave.

22. The "Spent A Lot" Spell

Tell your prospects that you have spent hundreds/thousands of dollars on different products but nothing ever worked this good. Your prospects most likely have spent tons of money on the same types of products too. That will help them relate to you and trust your judgment.

23. The "Biggest Benefit" Spell

Tell your prospects the best benefit that you have received from the product and how it improved your life. Your prospects might purchase the affiliate product if it's the biggest benefit that they need or want.

24. The "None Came Close" Spell

Tell your prospects you have tried a lot of products but none of them came close to this one. Your prospects have probably tried a lot of the same products but they haven't been exactly what they were looking for. They will hope that the affiliate product you are offering is finally the righ one.

25. The "Best Ever" Spell

Tell your prospects that the product has been one of your best investments ever. Your prospects will more likely be persuaded to order if they consider buying the affiliate product as an investment. They will feel they are getting money or something equal to money in return.

26. The "Not The Only One" Spell

Tell your prospects that you are not the only one that recommends the product and have them check out what other customers are say about it. Your prospects will believe you quicker if other people who have used the product are saying the same thing.

27. The "Similar Ones" Spell

Tell your prospects you have promoted a lot of similar products in the past but this product far exceeds them. Your prospects will appreciate the fact that you are saying this product is better than the other affiliate products you have promoted in the past. They will think it's really good, especially if they bought and liked the other products you've endorsed.

28. The "Crazy Or Not" Spell

Tell your prospects they would be crazy not to purchase the product. Your prospects will think it must be a good product because you are calling them crazy if they don't buy and you could lose money in the future insulting them that way.

29. The "Than It Promises" Spell

Tell your prospects that the product actually delivers more than the business promises. Your prospects like to hear about hidden benefits of a product that is not advertised on the sales page. It will give your prospects even more reasons to buy the affiliate product.

30. The "Outdone Themselves" Spell

Tell your prospects that you knew the business put out quality products but that they've outdone themselves this time. Your prospects like to do business with people that over-deliver on their product. They especially will like it if they know how reliable the business is before they release the new product.

31. The "Percentage Bribe" Spell

Tell your prospects that you will give them a percentage of your affiliate

commissions if they buy the product through your link. Your prospects will

relate it to getting a rebate for buying the product.

32. The "It's A Joke" Spell

Tell your prospects that comparing this product with other similar

products is a joke and why. Your prospects will be persuaded by you that

comparing the benefits of the affiliate product with a similar product just

doesn't stand up to it.

33. The "Long Term" Spell

Tell your prospects specifically how long ago you purchased the product

and all the long-term benefits you've gained and continue to receive. Your

prospects will be influenced to purchase the affiliate product because of

you telling them about all the long-term benefits that you have received

from it.

34. The "Another Scam?" Spell

Tell your prospects that before you bought the product you thought it was

just another scam, but that you were totally wrong. Your prospects have likely been scammed by other businesses in the past so they might feel the same way. They will be at ease that you have had similar experiences and maybe buy your affiliate product.

35. The "Pays For Itself" Spell

Tell your prospects that the product will pay for itself fast. Your prospects will buy an affiliate product quicker if you can show proof of how it has paid you back. They will want to get the same payback as you.

36. The "Scared Of Competition" Spell

Tell your prospects that you are scared to endorse the product because you don't want your competitors finding out about it. Your prospects will definitely think that they have to own the product because you are actually taking a big risk promoting it and they may be your competitors.

37. The "One Word" Spell

Tell your prospects it only takes one word for you to describe the product, for example, 'superb.' Your prospects won't have to spend a lot of time reading your affiliate offer for them to get the point. Just make sure the word is really persuasive.

38. The "Minutes Ago" Spell

Tell your prospects you just purchased and started using the product minutes/hours ago and you just had to tell them about it. Your prospects will think that the affiliate product has to be good because you couldn't wait to tell them about it.

39. The "Living Without It" Spell

Tell your prospects you don't know how you ever lived without the product and a good reason why. Your prospects will want to experience having a product that they can't live without because of all the benefits it offers.

40. The "Told Loved Ones" Spell

Tell your prospects that you are not only recommending the product to them but to your family members and close friends. Your prospects will really trust your offer because you are even endorsing it to the people you really, really care about.

41. The "Seconds Away" Spell

Tell your prospects it took you only seconds to buy the product because the product owner always delivers on their promises. Your prospects will think you have had good experiences with the business owner and their products and have never been displeased with any purchase from them.

42. The "Rarely Do" Spell

Tell your prospects you rarely endorse products but the product is astounding. Your prospects will think the affiliate product must be good i you are endorsing it. They will feel anyone that rarely endorses products is telling the truth.

43. The "Anyone Serious?" Spell

Tell your prospects that, in your opinion, anyone who is serious about gaining the benefits should buy the product. Your prospects are probably serious about improving their lives so they would be disagreeing with themselves if they didn't buy the affiliate product.

44. The "Use It A Lot" Spell

Tell your prospects you can't believe how much you actually use the product to get your desired benefits. Your prospects will feel they will get a lot of use out of the product. They want to own a product that they will actually use more than once.

45. The "Professional Opinion" Spell

Tell your prospects that, as a professional, you can't simply imagine a better investment and why. Your prospects will trust your offer more if you have the same profession as them or have a profession that is related to the affiliate product.

46. The "Take It With You" Spell

Tell your prospects you keep the product with you wherever you go. Your prospects will consider the affiliate product a requirement considering you always have it with you when you complete a certain action or project.

47. The "Honest Owner" Spell

Tell your prospects that, in your own opinion, the business owner is one of the most honest people you know. Your prospects will trust you because you are telling them your opinion and not actually trying to sway their opinion. They will also be more open to believing your statement because you actually know the business owner.

48. The "Recommend It Too" Spell

Tell your prospects that most people you talk to recommend the product too. Your prospects will usually agree with the majority. Most people like to use popular products and don't want to feel left out.

49. The "Barely Scratching" Spell

Tell your prospects you have barely scratched the surface of how great the product is. Your prospects will want to know the rest of the benefits of the product after you left them hanging for more. They will have to buy it in order to find out this mystery.

50. The "Biggest Complaint" Spell

Tell your prospects your biggest complaint about the product is that it wasn't available sooner. Your prospects will be a little confused because you're starting to complain but not actually about the product. Many people let down their buying defenses when they are confused.

51. The "Feel Sorry" Spell

Tell your prospects you feel sorry for those who don't believe what you are saying about the product. Your prospects will really think about

buying the affiliate product because
you're not directly selling to them but actually pitying them for "maybe"
not buying the product.

52. The "X's The Price" Spell

Tell your prospects that you told the business owner
that they are selling

the product far too cheap and you would have paid 10 times the price.

Your
prospects may want to hurry up and buy before the business owner

comes to their senses and raises the price.

53. The "Meet Me Halfway" Spell

Tell your prospects you will give them a 50% discount off any of your
own

products if they buy the product through your affiliate link. Your
prospects

would be highly persuaded to purchase the product if one of your

products could improve an aspect of their life.

54. The "Best Thing Since" Spell

Tell your prospects that you truly believe the product is the best thing

since a similar good product. Your
prospects will likely buy if you compare

the affiliate product to another product that has received good reviews
or

endorsements.

55. The "You Realize It Now" Spell

Tell your prospects you now know

that the product is as good as everyone says it is. Your prospects will see that you heard other people saying how good the affiliate product was and that persuaded you to purchase it. Your prospects now feel they are in the same position you were in.

56. The "Wasn't Sure" Spell

Tell your prospects you weren't sure whether to order the product at first but you're so happy you did. Your prospects are likely to think the same thing. They will be persuaded to buy because they will want to be happy also.

57. The "Jealousy" Spell

Tell your prospects that you are jealous of the business's new product. Your prospects will like the fact that you can openly admit it. They will want to buy it and see why you are jealous.

58. The "Seen It All" Spell

Tell your prospects that you thought you've heard and seen it all. Your prospects have likely said the same thing about other products at least once in their lives. They will be interested in seeing what all the fuss is about.

59. The "A Little Extra" Spell

Tell your prospects that you will give them some bonus products if they order the product through your affiliate link. They would have to be crazy

to order the product through another affiliate's link.

60. The "Long Time Ago" Spell

Tell your prospects you wished the business had created this product a long time ago. Your prospects have likely said that same thing about another product in the past. It will trigger them to feel that same feeling about your affiliate product.

61. The "Free Promotion" Spell

Tell your prospects you will give them a form of free advertising or a joint venture opportunity if they order the product through your affiliate link. A large percentage of people on the Internet have some type of business to promote.

62. The "Better Than Nothing" Spell

Tell your prospects that you will give them the next product you create (a future bonus) for free if they buy the product through your affiliate link. Your prospects will think at least that's better than ordering and getting zilch.

63. The "I'll Train You" Spell

Tell your prospects you will give them free advice, consulting or training using the product if they order it through your affiliate link. Your prospects will like the fact they won't have to learn how to use the product alone.

64. The "Right For You?" Spell

Tell your prospects you're not sure whether the product is right for them.

Your prospects will then want to find out if the affiliate product is right for them. They won't want to feel less of a person for not buying.

65. The "Made A Deal" Spell

Tell your prospects that you made a deal with the owner of the product to

give you a discount if they order through your affiliate link. Your

prospects will feel grateful that you are trying to save them some money.

66. The "Know From Experience" Spell

Tell your prospects you know from experience the product is what they've

been looking for. Your prospects will consider you somewhat of an expert

on the type of affiliate product you are recommending to them. They will

likely be persuaded quicker by someone who has had the same

experience as them.

67. The "Bought It Again" Spell

Tell your prospects the product works so good you almost bought it again.

Your prospects will be stunned by that statement and lower their buying

defenses. They will wonder who in their right mind would purchase a product again that didn't have too.

68. The "I Won't Sell It" Spell

Tell your prospects you wouldn't sell or get rid of the product for any price. Your prospects will think the affiliate product must be really valuable. They will think the product will give them benefits that can't be bought with money.

69. The "First To Hear" Spell

Tell your prospects you made a special deal with the business owner and they are the first to hear about the product. Your prospects may want to purchase the affiliate product before everyone else does. They will want to be one of the first people to experience the benefits.

70. The "Over And Over" Spell

Tell your prospects they will use the product over and over again. Your prospects will think if they will use the product multiple times, it will be worth the purchase price. Many people regret buying a product which they only use once then stick in the closet.

71. The "I Found It" Spell

Tell your prospects the product was just what you were looking for. Your prospects will have an idea or image of a product that they have been searching for. They will think the product is meant for them since you had a similar situation.

72. The "Higher Income" Spell

Tell your prospects that you made a deal with the owner of the product that if they buy the product through your affiliate link, they will get a higher commission rate if they sign up for the affiliate program.

73. The "Nothing Like It" Spell

Tell your prospects you've never seen any product like it. Your prospects want a product that will give them a breath of fresh air. They are always on the lookout for a different product that will give them better benefits.

74. The "I'd Be Shocked" Spell

Tell your prospects you would be shocked if they didn't at least make back their purchase price. Your prospects may justify buying the product because they can make their money back by joining the affiliate program.

75. The "Can Only Imagine" Spell

Tell your prospects you know what the product has done for you and you can only imagine what it will do for them. Your prospects will think the affiliate product will work even better for them since their situation may be worse.

76. The "Friends" Spell

Tell your prospects that you are friends with the business owner and have met and talked with him/her in person. Your prospects will trust buying the business's product through your affiliate link because you are putting

your reputation on the line for them.

77. The "One Word Reaction" Spell

Tell your prospects as soon as you used or saw the product, all you could say was 'Wow!' Your prospects have likely had a situation where they have used one word reactions to express their emotions. They will be persuaded to buy if they had some of those same reactions to other products in the past.

78. The "Done It Again" Spell

Tell your prospects the business owner has done it again. Your prospects will think the business owner has created another incredible product. They will also be persuaded to buy if you have bought from the same business in the past.

79. The "Can't Match It" Spell

Tell your prospects that there's not a product anywhere that can match the product. Your prospects will figure they might as well buy your affiliate product since there are no other products that can match it. They will think it will be the only product they will need in order to get their desired benefits.

80. The "Saw My Friend" Spell

Tell your prospects you have a confession to make and you weren't going to buy the product until you saw your friend benefiting from it. Your prospects will trust you more because you're showing the same feeling they are probably having at the moment. Now you just need to show them how you're benefiting from the product.

81. The "Stop Thinking" Spell

Tell your prospects to stop thinking about it and start to improve their life. Your prospects are sometimes persuaded by direct commands, especially if they already trust your recommendations. They will take the commands as motivation to improve their life.

82. The "Thumbs Up" Spell

Tell your prospects you give the product two thumbs up. Your prospects will likely know what "two thumbs up" mean. They will have a clear mental vision of what you are telling them and it may trigger a positive buying thought.

83. The "Diamond" Spell

Tell your prospects you compare the product to a diamond in the rough. Your prospects can be persuaded by comparisons of the product to others things that will help them understand how good the product is.

84. The "Opportunity" Spell

Tell your prospects the product has opened up lucrative opportunities for

you. Your prospects are always looking for good opportunities that will

improve their lives. Most people are persuaded by financial benefits.

85. The "Too Good" Spell

Tell your prospects the product is almost too good to be true! Your

prospects have likely read product advertisements that have sounded too

good to be true. They will like the fact that you have bought the product

and you have actually seen it is true.

86. The "Good Service" Spell

Tell your prospects the business's customer service was prompt, friendly

and answered your questions. Your prospects have likely had problems

with other businesses' customer services in the past. They will be

persuaded to buy if you have proved their customer service is excellent.

87. The "Bought Them All" Spell

Tell your prospects you bought all of the products out there and tell them

to save their money, this one is the best. Your prospects will see how

much you have invested in similar products. They will like the fact you

bought other products before buying this one and will also like the fact

you are trying to save them money.

88. The "Word Burst" Spell

Tell your prospects a burst of persuasive words that describe the product, like amazing, incredible, superb. Your prospects will be persuaded to buy

because you are using few words to describe your experience with the affiliate product and have less reason to turn your recommendation down.

89. The "Excited" Spell

Tell your prospects you are excited about the product. Your prospects will

have to register the emotion in their brain to understand it and it may

trigger a past memory when they felt that way about a product.

90. The "Physical Reaction" Spell

Tell your prospects the product sent chills up your spine. Your prospects

will have to remember a time when the same physical reaction happened

to them and it may trigger the same reaction about the product you are

recommending.

91. The "Owner Bonuses" Spell

Tell your prospects that you made a deal with the owner of the product to

give them some extra bonuses if they order through your affiliate link.

Your prospects will feel special that they are getting bonuses that other

customers aren't.

92. The "Sub It Up" Spell

Tell your prospects if they sign up as a sub-affiliate under you that you

made a deal with the owner of the product to increase their commissions.

They will make money and so will you without selling the affiliate product.

93. The "Won't Without It" Spell

Tell your prospects you don't know how they will ever benefit without the product. Your prospects will think they are missing a product that could be of use throughout their life to give them their desired benefits. They want to know why they couldn't benefit without it.

94. The "Honesty" Spell

Tell your prospects you honestly have used the product and highly recommend it. Your prospects can be persuaded by you just telling them up front that you are being honest. They will think you wouldn't want to ruin your business by lying about your experience with a product.

95. The "Just See It" Spell

Tell your prospects they have to see it to believe it. Your prospects sometimes don't believe what anyone says about a product. They will think it's like a challenge (which can be exciting for them) to buy the product and see for themselves.

96. The "You Won't Fail" Spell

Tell your prospects it's impossible for them to fail with the product. Your prospects want to avoid failing at getting their desired benefit or reaching their goals. They will also like it if the product comes with a guarantee.

97. The "Weird Sound" Spell

Tell your prospects, "All I can say about this is "Ahhhhhh!"" Your prospects have likely used a sound in the past to describe their reaction to a product. They will be persuaded to have the same reaction to your product endorsement because they will have to mentally register what the sound means.

98. The "All The Perks" Spell

Tell your prospects the benefits of the affiliate program and that you'll train them for free if they sign up as a sub-affiliate through your link. You could tell them about the tracking system, professional affiliate tools, the percentage of commissions, etc.

99. The "Fringe Benefits" Spell

Tell your prospects that the first 100 that order through your affiliate link will get a rebate, bonus or discount. If your prospects are even remotely interested, they will most likely jump at your offer because they don't want to lose the fringe benefits.

100. The "Divided And Conquer" Spell

Tell your prospects that you made a deal with the owner of the product that they can pay via a 3-month payment plan if they order through your link. The price of any product seems more affordable if it's divided up into payments.

Conclusion:

Now you can be a confident expert on promoting affiliate products. Ok, maybe not an expert. Keep in mind that any subject can change over time, so be sure you keep up with the latest news.

If you've picked some pointers about marketing affiliate products that you can put into action, then by all means, do so. You won't really be able to gain any benefits from your new knowledge if you don't use it.